BETTER THAN NEW

Douglas Hiller

LDA
LEARNING · DEVELOPMENT · AIDS

Better Than New
LD875V
ISBN 1 85503 015 2

Published under licence in the UK by LDA

First published in UK 1990

LDA, Duke Street, Wisbech, Cambs., PE13 2AE England

Printed in Great Britain by Ebenezer Baylis and Son Ltd,
The Trinity Press, Worcester, and London.

CHAPTER

1

Is Sally's Number Up?

It was no use. Sally Steele had no idea which number on the list was the number of the drawing she had to find. "Help," she said in a whisper. She felt like screaming the word, but of course she didn't. People didn't scream in electronics companies. And they certainly didn't make noise when they were in plenty of trouble already.

"What's wrong now?" Joe Harper asked from the desk next to Sally's.

"I just can't work it out," Sally told her friend with the long, black moustache and dark, kind eyes. "All these numbers look alike. I'll never remember the one for the drawing we need. I give up."

Let them sack me, Sally thought as she stared at her old grey desk. I won't blame them one bit. They hired a blockhead, and they might as well fire one. I hate numbers — and I'm plain-looking and clumsy to boot. "I don't know why I even get up in the morning," she said to Joe, trying to laugh.

Joe shook his head. "Take it easy, Sally," he told her. "You'll find it. Check the list again. And again if you have to. You'll find it, or it will come back to you. It's so much easier to find a drawing by its number. It could take us all night if we have to go through the folders one by one."

"All right," Sally said in a tired voice. "But I'm sure it's no use."

"What's that I hear about something taking all night?" Sally dropped her head closer to her list as she heard Edna Corwin's icy voice asking the question.

"We may have to work late," Joe told Edna as she came into the office. "One of the drawings on the Antel job was changed yesterday. Ms. Dodd asked to see it first thing tomorrow morning. And we're — ah — having a bit of trouble finding it."

"But this is our bowling night," Edna said in a voice that was used to getting its way. "You can't miss that." Then she looked at Sally in that special "what a mouse you are" way.

"Could it be that our little Sally is having trouble with the numbers again?"

Sally stared down at her list, trying to come up with a clever answer. As usual, none came.

Edna just shook her head at Sally. Then she thought for a moment. "You wouldn't be looking for the drawing you put through the copy machine yesterday? Remember? I was at the machine at the same time?"

"Yes, that's the one," Sally said. She looked up at Edna's "I knew I would figure it out" face.

"That was drawing 23227," Edna went on. I just happened to notice the number as it was coming out of the machine." Edna smiled down at Sally and started to straighten some papers on Sally's desk.

"Oh, thanks, Edna," Sally said gratefully. She was pleased at the thought of not having to hunt through the files all night. "What a wonderful memory you have. I wish mine was half as good."

"The difference, I think, is that I'm interested in my work." Edna spoke sharply as she started to walk out of the office.

"Big deal," Joe said once Edna had left the room. "She has a trick memory, that's all."

"It's more than that," Sally told him. "She does everything right. That's why everyone says she's going to be the next department head. And you know, she's right about my interest in this job, Joe. I don't like it, and I'm no good at it."

"Are you going bowling tonight?" Joe asked, changing the subject. "Judy wanted me to ask you."

"Of course," said Sally, smiling at the thought of spending time with her good friend, Joe's wife. "Maybe I don't like my job. But I do like bowling."

"You really do, don't you," Joe stated. He smiled a half-smile at Sally, then turned quickly to his work.

Sally sat very still for a moment, staring at Joe's face and the dark-brown glasses that hid his eyes. "Are you trying to tell me something?" she asked.

Her friend didn't look at her.

"Come on, Joe. I may be a bit of a blockhead, but even I know when you have something on your mind."

"It's about your bowling," he said, still studying his work.

"I know," Sally said. "Edna thinks I should practice more. Everyone on the team bowls better than I do. It's my fault that the team's score is low. But don't look so upset. I'll catch up."

Now Joe looked over at Sally. "The truth is, Edna wants you off the team. I'm afraid she even has someone to take your place already," he went on. "Someone from the Art Department. She plans to have the team vote on it at the alley tonight."

"Great," said Sally, leaning so far back in her chair it groaned. "Then that does it. I'm off the team. Even if Judy sides with me, the other two will side with Edna. What Edna wants, Edna gets. I guess that finishes my bowling."

"It doesn't have to. If you bowl three good games tonight, she won't be able to call for a vote.

"That's right," said Sally, smiling in a sad way. "But there's no chance of that happening is there?"

CHAPTER

2

Sally Gets the Blues

At eight o'clock that evening, Sally pulled into the bowling alley's car park. She parked her old Ford carefully, leaving plenty of room on both sides. She never felt in complete control of the dirty blue Ford, and it always gave her trouble.

"Just stay put," Sally said to the car. "And please start up when it's time to go." Then she started to cross the car park with her bowling bag.

Inside, Judy Harper saw her coming and waved quickly. "Over here," she called, making room for Sally on the seat. "Why are you so late? Edna and the others have already started their practice game."

"I almost didn't come," Sally said. She pulled off her street shoes and started hunting in her bag for her bowling shoes. "I guess Joe told you what might happen. I didn't want to face getting kicked off the team. Then I decided not to give up without a fight. Joe said if I bowled three good games, Edna couldn't call for a vote."

Sally stopped talking for a moment as one of the bowlers made a strike with a crashing noise. "So here I am," she finished, standing up to fish out her bowling ball. "Wish me luck. I'm going to need three very good scores."

But Sally didn't get them. Her best game was only 86. Her worst was 63.

"You should get a fur cover for your ball. That way you could dust the gutters while you play." Edna laughed when she spoke, but her eyes were mean and ugly.

Sally sat down after she had thrown her last ball and quietly began changing her shoes. In a moment, Edna came over and looked down at her. "I've been talking to the other team members," Edna said in a voice that everyone could hear.

"And?" Sally asked, looking right at her shoes. She knew what was coming, and she didn't want to hear it.

"When we started this team," Edna began, "We called for people who knew how to bowl. But it's clear to everyone — except you — that you don't know how."

Sally turned bright red, but she couldn't say a word. Her answer stuck at the back of her throat.

"So we took a vote," Edna went on. "You're off the team. We already have somebody to fill your place."

"Sure," Sally said, still not looking up. "I understand. The team comes first."

"No hard feelings," Edna said, smiling but walking away fast.

"No hard feelings," Sally repeated. But her voice was lost in the sound of pins hitting the floor and people laughing and sharing a good time. Judy came right up and sat down next to her. The two women watched the other bowlers quietly until Edna and her friends had gone.

"Are you OK?" Judy asked. "Joe and I tried to talk her out of it, but she wouldn't listen."

"I know," Sally told her friend. "I'm OK."

"I just wish there was some way to get even with Edna," Judy said in an angry voice.

"There isn't" Sally told her. "People like Edna don't get kicked off teams. They just go along right on top of things."

"Some day she'll get what's coming to her."

"I doubt it," Sally smiled. "But don't worry about it. Think about where we should meet for lunch next week instead."

After waving goodbye to Judy, Sally put on her sweater. Then she walked through the prize-lined rooms of Redwood Bowl. Stepping out into the night, she headed for her Ford. She let out a deep breath when the car started on only the third try. But it banged and popped like the angry, old machine it was. Sally was always afraid it would fall apart any second.

Driving slowly, she pulled out of the car park and onto the street. Everyone on the team is probably laughing at me, Sally thought. She felt awful. The car was a mess. Her job was a mess. She was a mess. Why didn't the world just stop so she could get off? She wished she could close her eyes and open them again a million miles away. But things like that didn't happen.

"Come on, car," Sally said. She had decided to take the short way home, even though Sherman Drive was very lonely. As she turned onto the drive, she saw a large circle of blue lights high in the sky, right above her.

What is that, she asked herself. Am I seeing things? She drove on, but the lights seemed to follow her. If she went fast, so did the lights. If she slowed down, the lights did too. "I think I'm going crazy," she said out loud.

Then the car's engine died. "It figures," Sally said. She stopped wondering about the lights and steered the Ford to the side of the road. Then she pulled on the brake, opened the door, and got out. She looked helplessly at the old blue wreck. "Why are you so awful? Why don't I have enough money to buy a new car? Why —" Sally kicked angrily at one of the front tyres.

Then she sat back down on the front seat. "This is great," she said. "Hardly anyone uses this road. There isn't a house in sight. And there is no way I'm going to walk home — I'd probably get lost." She shook her head. "Now there is nothing left that can go wrong today."

Suddenly she looked up. The circle of blue lights was still there. In fact, it seemed to be watching her, hanging in the sky just above her head.

A helicopter. It must be a police helicopter, Sally told herself. She waved at it. "Here I am," she called. At least she'd be able to get home now.

The lights began to move slowly down.

Finally some luck, Sally said to herself. This couldn't happen again in a million years. Then she took another look at the blue lights. They were closer now, and the craft they shone from suddenly didn't look much like a helicopter.

"What —?" Sally's heart began to pound as the flat, round craft moved toward her. She could see now that it was like nothing she had ever seen before. "It's — it's a UFO!" She screamed, turning to run from the shiny, green ship. But she was too late. A ray of white light shot out from the ship and hit her. Though still awake and seeing, Sally became as silent and still as her old Ford. She had no choice. The light from the ship had frozen her stiff as a board.

CHAPTER

3

In Good Hands

As Sally watched, the spaceship landed, filling the whole road. Then the blue lights changed to yellow, and a wide door opened in the side. Out stepped what Sally thought must be the pilot of the strange craft. But the thing — or animal — or whatever it was — was alarming to see.

It was round, like a giant ball, and covered with thick, blue hair. It had four eyes — but not on a face. The eyes peered out from the pilot's body. There were no ears or mouth that Sally could see. But she did see arms — 10 of them. Each ended in a hand with no fingers — just four thumbs.

The thing started moving toward Sally, walking on three of its arms. Then it put down two more to help it move faster. Sally would have screamed again if she could have. But she still couldn't move or speak. All she could do was stand there scared stiff as the blue creature came towards her.

"Don't be afraid." The creature hadn't said anything, but the words formed in Sally's head.

"What is this? Who are you?" Sally thought in return. It seemed as if thought waves were how the creature sent its messages.

The answer filled her mind. "I am Barzak. My job is to learn new things."

Dozens of questions came into Sally's head, far too many for Barzak to receive and answer all at once. "Save your questions," Barzak told her. "Right now, I have work to do."

The creature got behind Sally's old car and pushed it with several arms through the open door of the spaceship. Then it came back and picked up Sally. Fear filled her mind again, but a message told her not to worry. For some reason, Sally believed the message, and she stopped feeling afraid. Something made her know that Barzak was friendly and didn't plan to hurt her.

The strange pilot carried Sally into the ship and put her down in a room with a window. As

Sally looked through the window,she saw the light outside change from yellow to blue again. Then the ship rose into the night sky. There wasn't so much as a mark on the road to show where it had been.

The earth dropped away quickly. The stars became very bright, then turned into lines of light. But soon they too were gone. A thick, dark cloud had covered the ship.

Where in the world am I going? Sally wondered. This must be some kind of a crazy dream. Then Barzak came back into the room. And again Sally felt that no matter how crazy things were, they would turn out all right.

"That's right," Barzak said in Sally's mind, reading her thoughts again. "I won't hurt you. I wish only to study you and your car. It's my job to learn new things."

"Study me?" Sally looked up at the creature. "How?"

The answer formed in her mind.

"First I will take you apart . . . ."

CHAPTER

4

Better Than New

Barzak picked Sally up and placed her on a long table in the bright pink and yellow room. This is going to be interesting! Sally thought to herself. Blue light came down and covered her, making her skin feel cold. Then a wall opened up, and Sally could see strange tools hanging in the air behind it. Barzak picked one that looked like a pencil and began to work.

It removed Sally's arms and legs first. There was no blood when they came off, and nothing hurt. Sally was awake the whole time. Somehow she still wasn't afraid. She could only wonder at the strange goings-on.

Barzak worked in silence. The creature checked each of her arms and legs with several machines before setting it aside. Then it studied other parts of Sally's body. Sally followed everything perfectly. Even when her brain was placed in the machines, she knew what was going on. She could feel her memories being searched and studied like old papers in a file drawer.

When Barzak was finished, the creature put Sally back together again. This time it used a flat tool and a hammer. Then the blue creature pushed the Ford into the room and began taking it apart. Soon Barzak had the floor covered with pieces of the old car. Watching from her seat near the window, Sally couldn't imagine how the creature would get the Ford together again.

"I put you back together, didn't I?" Barzak said in Sally's mind, answering her thought. "After that, this simple machine will be no problem."

Sally would have smiled if she could have. Instead she went on watching Barzak. The blue creature didn't seem to tire, though it worked for hours. Finally, as Barzak had promised, the car was back in one piece. The Ford looked exactly as it had before Barzak had taken it apart.

The creature put away the tools and rubbed its arms with its 10 hands. Then it turned to Sally. "This has been very interesting," Barzak said in Sally's mind. "But there's something you should know. I've put you back together with a few changes. You're in better shape now than you were."

"What do you mean by a few changes?" Sally thought in anger. For the first time on the spaceship, she felt really afraid. "Am I going to turn blue like you? Or grow 10 arms? On earth, that's not better."

"The changes are not what you think," Barzak told her. "See for yourself."

There was a sudden flash of bright lights, and Sally was able to move again. She jumped up and tested her arms and legs. There were only two of each, and they seemed to be in working order. Her skin was the same colour too. Hard as she looked, there was nothing to show that she had been taken apart and put back together again.

But something *was* different. She felt better than she had ever felt before. She smiled and shook her head. "I'm OK. In fact, I feel better than new."

"It would be against the laws of my world to harm another life form" was Barzak's message. "Also, this is our way to pay others for helping us. I learned new things from you.

So I've thanked you by changing you to the way you've always wanted to be."

Barzak's message stopped for a second. Then it continued. "By the way, what does the word *Edna* mean?"

"Edna? It means nothing."

"Good," said Barzak. "That's what I thought."

Sally walked around the bright room, her mind racing. This is too much," she said. "Will I have a better memory? Will I be strong? And have more luck than I used to?"

"All that and more," Barzak answered.

"I can't believe it," Sally said, hugging herself. "But will I remember what happened to me here?"

"Of course. If I took your memory away, I would be harming you. I can't do that. But even though no one would ever believe you, I must ask you to keep this all a secret. If you tell, the gifts I have given you must be returned."

"Then the changes in me will last for the rest of my life?" Sally asked.

"Well, no. Only for 100 years," Barzak answered.

Sally laughed. "That's long enough. For 100 years of being better than new, I promise never to tell anyone about you or your spaceship." Sally would have shaken hands on the deal, but she didn't know which of Barzak's many hands to shake. Then she had a thought.

"How will I explain to people why I've been away so long?"

"You won't have to say anything. You've been away only a few minutes," Barzak said in Sally's mind.

"But how can that be? It took hours — maybe days — to take me and the car apart," Sally said.

"Time is not the same everywhere. Days on this ship and my world are, at most, only minutes on earth."

"Then let's not waste even one more minute of time," Sally said with a grin. "Home, Barzak."

CHAPTER

5

The New Model

Barzak landed the spaceship back in the middle of Sherman Drive. In a moment, the Ford had been pushed out onto the road. Sally headed toward it, watching the strange creature who had certainly put a sparkle into a really terrible day. She wished she knew more about where it had come from and what life was like there.

"No time now," Barzak told her. "It's time for you to do some catching up instead." Then blinking four eyes and waving five hands, Barzak returned to the ship and sent it slowly up into the night sky. Sally watched until the blue lights were lost behind their dark cloud.

What a night! Sally thought to herself as she got behind the wheel. Looking up at the empty sky, she turned the key to start the engine. What she heard made her jump. The engine sounded so smooth! It almost hummed! Barzak must have made a few changes for the better in her old car as well.

Now *that* was a real test of Barzak's powers! Sally thought.

She headed off, chin up. The two miles to her block of flats had never seemed shorter or nicer to drive. Before she knew it, she was there and parking the car.

The night was quiet as Sally started walking toward the front door. But in a moment, it was filled with barking. Sally turned and saw her neighbour, Mrs Hammer, walking her small dog. Though Sally had often walked him, Scotty was barking at her as if she was a stranger.

"Sally?" Mrs Hammer had an odd look on her face.

"Hello, Mrs Hammer," Sally said, "What's wrong with Scotty?"

"Sally, it *is* you!" Mrs Hammer stared at Sally in the light of the street lamp. Then she smiled. "For a minute, I thought it was someone different. It's your hair, isn't it? One of those new cuts, I suppose. It does wonders for you. You look like a different person."

Sally stared down at Scotty, who was pulling on his chain. "Scotty thinks I *am* a different person."

"Of course he doesn't," said Mrs Hammer. "He simply wants to tell you how nice you look."

Sally bent down to pet the dog. "Hello, Scotty," she said. Still the dog barked at her.

"Maybe it's your voice," said Mrs Hammer with a questioning look. "Have you been taking singing lessons? My dear, I can't get over what's happened to you."

When she went inside, Sally was met with even more surprise. Sheba, her cat, made a terrible noise when she saw her. Then quickly the animal ran under a chair to hide.

"Oh, Sheba, not you too," Sally called as she headed for the bedroom. I must look awfully different to scare my own cat, she thought.

But when she looked in the mirror, nothing seemed to have changed. The same Sally Steele that had looked back at her long ago that morning was looking back at her now. The same eyes, the same hair — everything the same. Yet somehow everything was different.

Sally looked at herself harder. Her eyes were still green — but they seemed brighter, clearer. Her hair was still the same old colour — but now it was thick and wavy, not thin and dull. She even seemed taller — maybe she was only carrying herself straighter. She looked — well, better, happier, *prouder.*

With a last look, Sally headed back to the living room. "Sheba," she called. "Come out, come out, wherever you are. Dinner time." But Sheba stayed put. Smart cat, Sally thought as she went into her tiny kitchen. She knows I'm not plain old Sally Steele any longer, the Sally who made a mess of everything. I'll have to make friends with Sheba all over again. But that's OK, Sally thought. She'll get to like the new Sally.

Getting Sheba's food, Sally felt she couldn't possibly sleep, even though the clock showed it was certainly time for bed. She was still too excited. She wanted to dance and sing, then climb back into her old brand-new Ford and race it to the moon. What a day! What a lot to think about.

But everything had not changed. There was still work tomorrow.

Work! Sally's heart jumped. How would she ever explain her new look and her new manner? Or her new ability to remember things. Barzak had promised her a better memory.

Think of all the dull numbers she would be able to remember now.

She changed her clothes and climbed into bed, still thinking about the next day. Then a magazine on the bedside table caught her eye. I wonder how much I can really remember now? She thought. I'll pick out one sentence and memorize it. She checked the clock. I'll see how long it takes.

She read the sentence in a few seconds. Then she closed her eyes. Printed on her memory, word for word, was the whole sentence. All right! thought Sally. Now for a bigger test. I'll try 10 sentences. In less than a minute, she had learned every word in every sentence by heart.

Sally's eyes flashed open. "This is impossible!" she said out loud. Then a small smile crossed her face. Hopping out of bed, she picked up the *A* book of her encyclopaedia set. Before the little hand on her clock had moved from 12 half-way to 1, she had read it through. Then she closed her eyes. The complete book raced through her mind, all in the right order.

CHAPTER

6

Sally Gives Someone a Lift

Dressing in a bright skirt and sweater the next morning, Sally worked out her plan. She would be on time to work today for sure — in fact, she would be the first one in. She would catch up on all her work. And then she would quit.

Pleased but still surprised at the smart-looking woman who peered at her from the mirror, Sally worked on her speech. "I quit, Edna," she said to the mirror. She stopped to let that sink in. "That's what I said, Edna. I quit."

Then she faced the lamp and threw back her shoulders. "I quit, Ms Dodd. This is really a very dull job. I know all the numbers by heart now, and I still don't like them. No, I don't know what I want to do with my life. But I do know this much. I don't want to spend one more day in this office."

The Ford was waiting for her in the street, looking as old and tired as ever. "But you're a tiger inside," she told it, getting behind the wheel. "A real tiger. And if Barzak promised me 100 years, I bet that goes for you too."

Sally pulled out onto the road, and headed straight for Sherman Drive again, to see the place where her life had been changed. As the trees and blue sky rolled by, she reached down and turned on the radio. Strange music filled the car, and she hit the horn in surprise. But then Sally laughed. The radio must have been tuned to Barzak's favourite station.

In a moment, she made the sharp turn onto Sherman Drive. And then she had to turn quickly again. A car was parked there, not quite off the road. It looked as if the driver had stopped to change a tyre.

"Of all places," Sally said, slowing down. Then she looked closer. The car was leaning badly to one side. The driver was nowhere in sight.

She stopped her car. What was that strange sound? Was someone groaning? Quickly Sally drove the Ford off the road and parked. Then she ran back and saw at once what had happened. A man *had* been changing a tyre. But the jack had slipped. Now the man's leg was pinned under the left back wheel.

"Help me," he groaned when he saw Sally. "My leg. I think it's broken."

"OK, just take it easy," Sally said. She was surprised at how calm and sure of herself she felt. "I'll get the jack working."

"It broke." The man was in great pain — that much was clear. "There's a CB in the car," he managed to say. "Call for help."

Sally got hold of the police right away. Then she came back to calm the man. "The police promised to get help here fast," she told him. He tried to nod, but instead he let out another groan.

Sally remembered a pillow in her car and brought it to put under the man's head. But it didn't seem to help much. Then, as she stared at the car, an odd feeling came over her. There *was* something more she could do. It just suddenly seemed as if she could lift the car and set the man free.

Sally shook her head. Impossible. What a crazy idea. A good memory, yes. But lifting cars? She tried to put the thought out of her head, but it wouldn't leave. Suddenly she stood up. "You know what?" she told the man. "I'm going to lift the car and roll it forward about a foot or two."

A look of fear flashed across the man's face. "Lift the car? Are you crazy?"

"I'm going to give it a try."

"Hey, don't," he cried, "You're nuts. You'll just drop it on me again. Don't touch it! You'll only make it worse."

"Trust me," Sally said. She opened the door and released the brake. Then she sized up the car — a really heavy Rover. She took a deep breath. It *was* impossible, but she knew she could do it. She bent her knees and took hold of the rear bumper. One, two, three, lift. The car went up in her hands, and she rolled it forward a few feet. Then she let it down slowly.

"A piece of cake," she told the driver, shaking her head and grinning. "You should feel a little better now."

The man stared at Sally, his mouth wide open. Then he groaned once and fainted dead away.

Sally started forward to help him again, but suddenly she heard the sound of a police car. She knew no one would believe what she had just done. Since the driver was safe now, it was probably best for her to just leave. She raced to the Ford and took off, laughing to herself. No one would believe her — but no one was going to believe the driver either. The police wouldn't even believe that his car had pinned him down. How could a car jump up and move from here to there? It was all a bad dream they would say.

Except, of course, for the man's broken leg. Oh well, Sally said to herself. I can't take care of everything.

* * *

Sally arrived at work five minutes late. Edna, of course, was in the office to meet her. She had put on her best department head look. "Why, Sally," she said. "I suppose you got up early just to practice coming in late." Then she stopped and stared at Sally. "What happened to your hair? Did you cut it? It — you — *something* looks different." She stared for a few seconds longer. Then with a sniff, she said, "I don't think it suits you at all."

"I like it," Joe called out. His eyes were smiling behind his thick glasses. "You look wonderful, Sally."

Edna turned to him. "What do you know, anyway?"

As Edna spoke, Sally stepped around her and went to sit at her own desk. It was piled high with papers. "Is Ms. Dodd in?" she asked Edna, who had followed her over. "I'd like to see her when she gets a chance."

"Stay away from Ms. Dodd," Edna told her, making a wave with her hand. "She is too busy to see anyone."

That did it. "I'll see her at noon," Sally said. Looking away from Edna, she began to go through her papers one by one. She would finish everything by noon and quit.

"I wouldn't go in there at all," Edna called over her shoulder as she left the room. "She's out to get you. She's been in an angry mood ever since she got in. Of course, you wouldn't know about that. But some of the drawings are mixed up. She thinks it's your fault."

"I'm sure it's not your fault," Joe said to Sally in an angry voice. "It was probably Edna's fault. She just knows how to point the blame."

Sally shook her head and grinned. "Thanks, Joe. But if the drawings are mixed up, I probably did it."

"You're too hard on yourself," Joe said. "You can do a lot if you'll only give yourself a chance."

Sally answered Joe with a steady smile. "You're a good person, Joe. A lot nicer and more understanding than some people around here. If it were up to me, you'd be made department head."

"Small chance of that," Joe said.

The morning went by slowly. But by noon, Sally's desk was cleared of papers. Holding her head up, she went to Ms. Dodd's office and knocked on the door.

"Come in."

Sally opened the door and walked in. Ms. Dodd was bent over her desk, a small light shining on her work. She did not even bother to raise her head. Instead she just said, "Yes? Yes?" And her pencil flew.

"Ms Dodd," Sally said.

There was no answer. "Ms. Dodd," Sally started again, this time more strongly. "I'm leaving," she added in a bright voice. For some reason, she was no longer nervous.

"Oh?" Finally Ms. Dodd looked up. She blinked twice as though she wasn't quite sure who was there.

"You're leaving? Too bad." She held up a piece of paper, then went on with a half-smile. "I was just going to give you a list of drawing numbers to forget."

Sally returned the half-smile with a whole one. She took the list, read it through once, and handed it back. Then she snapped out every number on the list and the job each drawing was part of.

Ms. Dodd blinked again. "You are Sally Steele, aren't you?" she said. She looked at Sally with the same odd look that Mrs Hammer had had the night before. "I don't understand. Edna always tells me you can't remember anything for more than two minutes."

Sally laughed. "As you can see, all that has changed. But there's someone who will never change — and that's Edna."

"Why should she change?" Ms. Dodd wanted to know. She had leaned back in her chair and was looking hard at Sally.

Sally took a deep breath. "She should change because she's only out for herself." Sally began. "She uses people and walks all over them. Sure, she's clever. But there's no one in the office who likes to work with her. Everyone is afraid of her."

"Is that so?" Ms. Dodd asked.

"Yes," Sally answered. "If you make her department head, the whole office will fall apart — or everyone will walk out. I'll be leaving, so it makes no difference to me. But I wanted you to know, because it should make a difference to you."

Ms. Dodd looked at Sally, not wanting to believe her but finding herself unsure. "And just who do you think should be department head, Ms. Steele?"

"Joe Harper," Sally answered. "He is as clever as Edna — probably more clever — and everyone can work with him."

"I see,"Ms. Dodd told Sally, a look of disbelief still on her face. "Well, I'll look into it."

Sally left Ms. Dodd's office quickly and leaned on the closed door once she was on the outside. I did it. She smiled to herself. Oh, Barzak, I did it.

After lunch, Sally told Joe about quitting. He didn't blame her, he said, and he made her promise to see him and Judy often. During the afternoon, Sally heard Ms. Dodd call in all the people in the office one by one. Sally couldn't quite believe that her words had carried so much weight.

Then the impossible happened. At four o'clock, Joe was called into Ms. Dodd's office. When he came out he was smiling. "Have I got something to tell you!" he whispered to Sally.

Sally smiled. "I think I already know what it is."

Joe's eyes were sparkling as he picked up the phone to call Judy.

At five o'clock, Sally began packing up the few things in her desk. Edna came by with her last cheque, smiling a queen-like smile. "Too bad you're leaving," she said. "You won't find another job so fast."

Sally took the cheque and just smiled back. She would give Edna the last word. The "perfect" person had a big surprise in store for her. And for the first time, Sally felt sorry for Edna Corwin.

CHAPTER

7

Better Than Old

Sally was happy to be free of her dull job. She almost floated down the street as she walked to her car, smiling at every person who hurried by. Then she decided to drive to the bank and cash her cheque so she could shop over the weekend. She also wanted to pick up a little treat for her frightened cat.

She reached the bank, parked the Ford and walked over to the side door. But as she pushed it open, a man backed out, forcing her away. He had a gun in one hand and a cloth bag in the other. Sally didn't have to be Sherlock Holmes to work out what was going on. The bank had just been robbed, and the man backing into her was the thief.

As soon as he saw Sally, the robber pointed his gun at her. "You got a car?" he asked.

Sally nodded. She couldn't take her eyes off the gun.

"Well, where is it? Where is it?" the man yelled. He pushed Sally ahead of him.

Sally shook her head to clear it. Then she turned and led the man straight to her car. But when he saw the old Ford, he stopped dead in his tracks. A funny look spread over his face, as if he were thinking it might be easier to get away on the bus. He pointed toward the car with his gun and asked, "Does it run?"

"Of course." Sally answered with far more force than she could have managed the day before.

"OK, get in then. You drive," the man ordered. He waved Sally into the front. Then he climbed into the back seat.

Smoothly and calmly, Sally pulled out of the car park and headed north. As she drove away, she could hear police cars coming from every direction.

"The police are coming," she said.

"No kidding. What did you think was going to happen? I just robbed a bank."

The man spoke roughly, but he seemed nervous. He ran his fingers quickly through his hair. Part of the hair was left standing straight up, and Sally could see it in the mirror. She couldn't believe she felt like laughing with a gun-waving robber in her back seat.

"OK, slow down now," the man told Sally. "We're away from the bank. Maybe we won't be spotted if we're not roaring around. After all, who would guess I would be in an old car like this?"

Sally slowed down. Then she decided to say what was on her mind. "You know, if this is the first time you've done anything like this, you should give yourself up. The court might not be too hard on you."

"I've robbed six banks," the man said, looking out of the back window.

"Well . . . if you had a good reason for —"

The man broke in, "You mean like wanting money but not wanting to work for it?"

"That isn't what I had in mind," Sally said.

A laugh roared out of the back seat.

"I didn't think so," the man told her.

Suddenly a police car came toward them, heading for the bank. It passed, then pulled to a stop and turned around to follow them. Lights flashing, it was moving fast.

"OK, lady," the thief said. "You better make this old machine fly."

Sally pressed her foot on the accelerator, taking the car up to 50, then 60. The police car stayed right behind them, and surprised drivers pulled to the side to let the two cars race by. Soon the city streets led into open road.

"Faster! Faster!" the man yelled. He saw that the blue and white police car was still hanging on. Sally took the Ford up to 70, then 80. The needle moved further and further to the right.

Suddenly the thief yelled out, "They're falling back!" Then he looked at Sally. "What kind of a car *is* this?"

"A Ford." Sally said.

"Come on, you know what I mean. There's no way a plain Ford could be so fast. Or so quiet. What did you do to it?"

"It's been — ah — fixed up with new parts and things. It's like new," Sally explained.

"You'll have to come up with something better than that," the man said. "The car wasn't this good even when it was brand-new."

Then the man started up from his seat. A number of police cars were suddenly in front of them, blocking the road.

"Go around them!" the man ordered. "No, go through them. I'll just bet this old car can do it." He put his head down to get ready for the crash.

But there wasn't any crash. Instead of following orders, Sally had taken her foot off the accelerator and put it on the brake. The car stopped abruptly, and the thief came flying over the front seat. Sally's hand flashed across the space between them. She grabbed the gun as it flew over the seat with the man.

"Why did you do that?" he wanted to know. He rubbed his head with one hand while trying to reach for his gun with the other.

"Because I'm tired of you," Sally said. "And I don't want to talk to you any more. But the police do." Sally threw open her door and ran toward the police cars, her hands above her head.

After a lot of explaining, the thief was taken away and Sally was free to go. But before she could drive away, one of the police officers came over to speak to her again.

"Listen," the woman said, as she ran a hand over Sally's old blue car. "We had a lot of trouble keeping up with you. Just what kind of car is this old thing anyway?"

Sally flashed her bright smile as she started the smooth engine. "Oh, just a Ford," she said.

CHAPTER

8

Into Something New

It was well after dark when Sally reached home. But she did not feel tired at all. It looked as if her better-than-new body needed less sleep than her old body had been used to.

So what could she do to fill all the new hours she would have? She could read 15 or 20 books a night. She could learn Spanish, French and German. She could . . . .

But then Sally remembered that filling the night hours wasn't her only problem. She no longer had a job. She would have to find something to fill the day hours too.

The more Sally thought, the more she knew that she wanted her new life to be interesting and exciting. She could probably learn to do anything she wanted in a couple of weeks. But once learnt, would it still be fun and fulfilling for her?

Sally walked around her living room thinking. Every now and then, she walked into the bedroom, looked in the mirror, and shook her head. Finally she grabbed a coat and headed for her car. She would poke around the night streets of the city to see if anything gave her an idea of what to do with her life.

She drove and drove, looking up at the tall buildings and watching the people walk by. Soon, she was in a part of the city she had never been in before. It was full of old buildings and gardens covered with weeds.

One small building had several newspapers lying by the door. Nobody lives there any more, Sally thought as she drove slowly by. But then she saw a small light inside. It slid across a window for only a second, and then it was gone.

Was someone breaking in? Sally parked her car and walked back to the house. She thought of calling the police. But they would only wonder what *she* was doing hanging around dark streets. She wondered a little herself as she went around the side of the building. She was looking to see how the other person had got inside.

She found the answer fast enough — an open window. Sally climbed inside, being careful not to make any noise. It was very dark there, but somehow her eyes adjusted right away. Then she made her way quietly toward the front of the house.

In the living room, Sally could just see the shape of a man sitting at the window. His back was to her as she spoke. "What are you doing here?" she said. She sounded as though she was just meeting a friend on the street.

"I could ask you the same question," the man said quietly. To Sally's surprise, he didn't make a move.

"I'm stopping a robbery," Sally told him. "I saw someone sneaking around in here."

"You must have seen yourself," the man said. He still didn't get up or look away from the window.

"Look," said Sally. She was getting angry at the man's manner. Tell me what's going on here, or I'll call the police."

Finally the man turned toward her. "Oh, let me call," he said, smiling. "I own the place."

Sally felt her face grow hot.

"Oh, I'm sorry," she said. "I'm new to this crime business."

"Are you sorry you broke in or sorry I own the building?" he asked. "Sometimes *I'm* sorry

I own it — it's such a mess. I haven't had time to do it up yet."

"I'm sorry I broke in," Sally said. "But I thought —"

"I know what you thought," the man said, turning back to the window. "You saw a dark house where no one should have been. Then you saw the light I foolishly turned on for a second. You thought — robber! So you came in through the open window on the side."

"This is crazy,"Sally said. "It sounds like I walked into a detective story."

"Guess what?" the man said. "You did."

CHAPTER

9

The Costa Crime

"Great!" Sally said excitedly. She pulled up a chair and sat down. "Exactly what are you doing? What's the case?"

The detective shook his head. "Wait a minute! You sound as if you want to work for me."

"Of course not," Sally answered. But then more words popped out, surprising her. "I don't want to work *for* you. But I might want to work *with* you." Then she thought, Barzak, what have you done to me?

"This is really silly," the man said. "You break into my house, think I'm a thief, and come up behind me in the dark. Then 10 minutes later, you want to be my partner. Lady, you don't even know my name."

"It's Jason Golden," Sally said.

For the first time, the man seemed really

surprised. He tried to look more closely at Sally in the dim light from the street.

"I don't know you, do I? We've never met, have we?" the detective asked.

"No,I don't think so," Sally told him.

"Then how do you know my name?"

"You mean a great detective like you can't work that out?" Sally tried not to laugh.

"I'm sure I could," he said. "But why don't you save me the trouble."

"OK. It's simple. Jason Golden is the name on the doorbell outside this building, If you own the building, the bell is yours. I happened to look at the name as I went past."

"And you remembered it?"

"Sure. I don't forget things."

"Never?"

"Never," Sally said. She shook her head clear of the giant list of numbers that had just jumped into it.

"How many newspapers are outside the front door?" Jason asked. "Let's have a little test."

"Five," Sally said quickly.

"What's the name on the papers?"

"The Telegraph-Journal."

"What colour is the letter box?"

"Tired office grey, just like the rest of the building — and like one I'm glad I'll never see again."

"What is the house number?"

"Two-three-two."

"That's pretty good," Jason said, nodding his head. "I'll have to give you that."

"Fine," Sally said. "I've answered your questions. Now answer mine. What's going on here? A partner shouldn't keep so many secrets."

"Not so fast. Tell me who you are first so I'll know if I should trust you."

"My name is Sally Steele. I'm 26, brave, loyal, and looking for an interesting new job. I hadn't thought about being a detective, but I'd like to try it. It looks as if it might be interesting. It might even be fun."

"It's interesting, that's for sure," Jason told her. "But it's not always fun — like sitting here in a dark room all night. You don't always get paid on time either. And there's often lots of danger."

"I know all that," Sally said with a laugh. "I watch TV."

Jason shook his head, then was silent for a moment. He turned back toward the window. "You have a nice voice," he said. "I like to think

I can tell what people are like by their voices. I guess I can tell you what I'm doing here if you really want to know." He cleared his throat. "Did you ever hear the name William Costa?"

"No."

"Well, he's wanted by the police everywhere," Jason went on. "He's killed four people. And his wife just happens to live right across the street."

"And you're waiting for him to visit her so you can grab him?"

"That's right. Him and the rewards for him. Altogether the rewards come to nearly £100,000," Jason said.

"How do you plan to catch such a dangerous man?" Sally asked.

"I don't plan to do it myself," Jason explained. "All I plan to do is call the police when I see Costa coming. They'll do all the work, and I'll get all the money for feeding them the word."

"Change of plan," a voice suddenly said out of the dark. "No one's going to be calling the police. And no one's going to be getting any money."

CHAPTER

10

Costa Sees the Light

"Costa?" Jason said softly.

"Right," came the answer.

"How did you know I was watching for you?"

"It wasn't too hard," the man answered. He had a big, deep voice that sounded as if it was coming from the bottom of a barrel. "I've kept away from my house for six months. But I call my wife now and then. She said there's been a stranger in the neighbourhood lately watching the house. I hung around on the street till I saw a flash of light in here. Then this lady parked down the street and climbed in through a window. That was more than enough. I followed her to find out what was going on."

"And then you heard us talking," Jason said.

"I sure did. But there's one more thing I want to hear you say." Costa came out of the dark and moved toward the dim light in the front of the room. In his right hand, Jason and Sally could see a gun that was large and ugly. "That's goodbye. Now which one of you wants to say it first?"

"Wait, wait," Sally said quickly. "I've never even seen what Jason looks like, Mr Costa. And he's never seen me. We were going to work together. Can't we at least turn the lights on for a second so we'll know who we might have been partners with?"

Costa was silent for a moment. Then he laughed. "It's a good try at putting all this off. But why not? I shoot better in the light."

"The switch is on the right, near the door," Jason told him.

"OK, OK. But don't try anything," Costa said as he backed toward the door. "I have you both covered."

Suddenly the room was filled with light. Jason and Costa both blinked. But thanks to Barzak, Sally's eyes didn't mind the change. She grabbed the nearest thing — a chair — and threw it hard at Costa. The chair knocked the gun from his hand, giving Jason a chance to jump the man. As the two rolled on the floor, Sally found a heavy lamp and smashed it down on Costa's head. He groaned, and then he lay still.

"Are you OK?" Sally asked her new friend as he slowly stood up.

"I think so. Now that Hurricane Sally has finished her act." Jason rubbed his arm and looked at Sally. "That was quick thinking, you know."

Sally found the torch and then the gun.

"And quick eyes too. I just may need a partner after all, if that's what you really want." He looked around for something to tie Costa up with as Sally answered.

"I'm not sure," she said. "But I'd like to try it for a while." Sally looked at the red-haired detective, then at Costa lying in the middle of the dark green rug that covered the floor. "It's been very exciting so far."

"Fine with me, partner," Jason told her. "When can you start?"

"Today's Friday. How about Monday? I can work all week except for Thursday evening. I already have plans for then."

"Sounds good," Jason said. He finished tying up Costa. As he picked up the phone to call the police he handed Sally his business card.

Sally headed for the door. "I want to be gone when the police get here."

"Oh, no," Jason said, putting the phone to his shoulder. "Don't tell me my new partner is in trouble with the police! I thought I could trust you."

Sally laughed. "You can. It's just that I caught a bank robber today — or yesterday now. I've answered enough questions for now. This time it's your turn to talk to the police."

"OK," Jason smiled. "As long as you call them the next time."

CHAPTER

11

A "Big" Case

On Monday morning, Sally found her way to Jason Golden's office. "I'm here, partner, she said. She pulled up a chair and sat down. "What's on for today?"

Jason pointed to some papers spread across his desk. "Well, no more Costas to be grabbed, I'm afraid. A wife wants us to follow her husband. A husband wants us to follow his wife. A missing person needs to be found. A lot of watching and waiting."

Sally made a face. She had been hoping for something more exciting. "Where are all the great puzzles that detectives are supposed to solve?"

"They're around. And they'll show up in our doorway sooner or later," said Jason.

"Looks like sooner," Sally said with a smile as she caught sight of someone at the open door. There stood a tall woman with straight blonde hair. She wore large, dark glasses and was dressed all in black. She was big, and she looked as if she meant business.

Wasting no time, the woman marched quickly into the office. "You're Jason Golden," she stated, standing before his desk.

"What can I do for you?" Jason asked.

"You're the cowboy who landed Costa." The woman's voice was strong, with just a touch of the North in it. "I need somebody like you to handle a little problem for me."

Jason pointed to a chair. "Have a seat. This is my partner, Sally Steele."

The woman looked over at Sally, then sat down abruptly and began speaking in a rush. "My name is Lizzie Sloane. I just bought myself a sweet little restaurant near Roden Drive. I call it Lizzie's Place. It cost me an arm and a leg. All hard-earned money too. But I'm still willing to pay a pretty penny to have a couple of crooks put behind bars."

"Wait, hold everything," Sally said. "What did these people do?"

Lizzie Sloane turned slowly toward Sally and looked her up and down. "They want protection money from me, the —" She stopped herself and looked back at Jason. "But they won't get anything from me."

"I see," said Jason. "Now what —?"

"You don't see anything," Lizzie broke in. She pulled her glasses off. Her pale blue eyes were hard but worried. "I buy a beautiful restaurant. I do it up really nice. Then I open to big crowds. Everyone loves the place. And that's when the trouble begins. In walk these two crooks. 'Nice place you have,' they tell me.

" 'I like it,' I say.

" 'It would be too bad if something happened to it,' they say.

" 'Nothing is going to happen,' I tell them.

" 'You never know', they tell me. 'But £1,000 a week should keep it safe and sound.' "

Lizzie stopped for a second, her face red with anger. "I told them to get out and not come back. They just laughed."

She put her glasses back on. "Golden, I want you to help me put an end to this protection game."

"I don't know," Jason said. "It looks like a matter for the police. When those guys come back for the cash, just hand them over to the cops. I don't see your problem."

Sally made a face. Jason was turning down an exciting job — one that sounded a lot more interesting than following people around.

But Lizzie wasn't to be turned down. "I thought you'd be smarter than that, Golden," she said. "Sure, it would be easy for the police to grab them when they come in again. But I want to catch a bigger fish. When those guys were in my place, I heard them talk about a Mr Big."

"Come on," Jason broke in. "Mr Big?"

"I know," said Lizzie. "Hard to believe, but the name *was* Mr Big. Anyway, they didn't know I heard them talking about him. And it seems he works this protection game up and down the coast. I want you to find Mr Big — by following those two guys — and let me know where he is. Then I'm going to give him a pay-off he won't forget."

"Wait a minute," Sally said carefully. "We're in the detective business, not the murder business."

Lizzie gave a loud laugh. "Murder? I'm not going to kill him. I'm just going to hand him over to the police in a few small pieces."

"Will you set up a pay-off time then?" Jason asked.

Lizzie smiled. "Looks like you're hooked. Yes, I'll tell those jerks to show up for their money around seven tomorrow night. And speaking of money, let's get down to business. I'll pay you £200 a day."

"£400 a day," Sally snapped back.

Jason tried hard not to smile as Lizzie threw Sally a terrible look. But then the tough hard-talking lady broke into another loud laugh.

"Well, sure!" she said. "Why not? Suit yourself." She gave them the address of her restaurant. "As I said, I'll get my visitors to show up there around seven tomorrow. Be there at six, and I'll give you a free meal with all the trimmings." Then, as fast as Lizzie Sloane had come in, she walked out.

Jason and Sally sat for a moment in the sudden quiet. "Well, that was something," Jason finally said. "The only problem is, I think Ms. Sloane really means to do our Mr Big in, not just turn him in."

Sally nodded. "We'll just give him to the police before our friend can get her hands on him."

CHAPTER

12

The Mercedes Twins

Lizzie's Place was already crowded when Sally and Jason got there at six on Tuesday. As the two detectives sat at their table waiting for Lizzie, they could see plates of wonderful-looking food going by.

"Who would figure that a tough customer like Lizzie would own a smart restaurant like this," Sally remarked in a low voice.

Soon Lizzie came toward them, flashing a proud smile. "What do you think of my place?" she asked.

"It's great," said Jason. "But let's get down to business. It'll be seven before we know it." He reached for a piece of bread. "I'll stay here to see that there's no trouble when Ms. Sloane hands over the money. Sally, you wait in the Ford to see what kind of car those guys drive up in. When the money has been passed, I'll join you. And we'll tail Mr Big's helpers right to him. Any questions?"

Sally started to say something in an angry voice, but Lizzie broke in. "Hold it one minute! Could the Ford you're talking about be that tin can I see outside the window? You won't get too far in that pile of junk!"

"Take it easy," Sally said. "There's no reason for you to get so upset. That car is a tiger. Don't let its looks fool you." Then she turned to Jason. "But there is a reason for *me* to get upset. Why is it you get to stay inside having a great dinner while I go outside with an empty stomach to wait in the car?"

Jason smiled. "Because I've been a detective longer — and because it's such a good plan." Then he handed Sally a piece of bread. "Here. Now you won't go hungry."

Talking under her breath, Sally headed for the Ford. But she didn't have long to stew. At seven on the dot, a long, black Mercedes pulled up in front of the restaurant. Two men stepped out. Sally saw a gun flash under one of the coats. She whistled, but not because of the gun. The two men looked exactly alike. They were twins!

The men stayed in the restaurant more than 10 minutes. When they came out again, Jason followed. As the twins headed for their car, Jason climbed into the Ford.

"Those are our boys," he said, nodding at the two brothers. "Lizzie handed over the money, but I could see she wanted to wrap her fingers around their necks."

In a moment, the Mercedes pulled out onto the road. It moved slowly, as if the men inside were sure no one would try to follow them. But Sally and Jason were right on their tail. From Lizzie's Place to Café Pierre to another restaurant and then another. Finally the pick-ups for the day must have been finished, and the Mercedes drove to a small, white house near the beach. The twins went in and stayed. After an hour, Sally and Jason left.

On Wednesday the two detectives were ready to spend another day following the twins. They had already found out that their name was Spark and that they had no record. As Sally and Jason started to tail the Mercedes down the street, they were surprised to see another Mercedes fall in behind it.

"This is it! There's going to be a drop somewhere," said Jason excitedly. "Mr Big must be in the second car. Don't lose him!"

"No chance of that," said Sally as she pressed her foot down on the accelerator. But instead of starting, the Ford just made a terrible noise.

"Hey, Tiger," Sally said. "You're not supposed to do that."

Jason looked worried as the Mercedes pulled away. "I thought you trusted this car."

"It's supposed to last 100 years," Sally said.

"Who told you that? The clown at your garage?"

"More or less," said Sally, picturing the 10-armed "clown". She accelerated again, and this time the Ford moved out. But it still didn't sound right.

"At least it's going," Jason said. "If some clown told you this car would last 100 years, he doesn't know cars. I'd say he probably doesn't know his right hand from his left."

"You can say that again!" Sally laughed.

Soon, however, the Ford was making strange noises again, and Sally had to pull over to the side of the road. But just ahead of them, the two Mercedes had stopped by another restaurant. Sally and Jason each let out a deep breath as the Spark twins made their way toward it.

"We're in luck." Jason jumped out of the car. "I'll check the dipstick," he said.

His words rang a bell in Sally's head. "That's it!" she said. "I'll bet it's out of oil."

For a moment, she was surprised she hadn't remembered to check the oil before. Then she thought of the extra can she always carried in the back. Quickly she found it and poured it in.

They were ready to go when the Mercedes pulled away again. Soon all three cars were on the motorway leading out of the city. Though the awful noise had stopped, Sally was still worried about her car. It just didn't seem to handle right.

The Mercedes soon turned off the highway and onto a two-lane road. Sally followed, keeping back, as the trees along the road changed into deep forest. Then all of a sudden, both Mercedes slowed down. Sally looked in the mirror. There was not another car to be seen. She and Jason were alone with the two Mercedes in the middle of nowhere. She began to slow down too.

"What are these guys up to?" Jason asked, leaning forward. "This could be the drop, or they could have figured out what *we're* up to."

The answer came right away. The Mercedes turned around and headed straight for the old Ford. Quickly it was sandwiched between the larger cars. There was nothing Sally could do but step on the brakes.

CHAPTER

13

Close Call

Sally and Jason wasted no time in getting out of the Ford. The two men pointing guns at them looked like they meant business.

"Over there," one man said. "Our boss wants a word with you." He waved Sally and Jason toward the second Mercedes.

The back door was opened, and Sally was pushed inside. Jason came crashing in after her. When they righted themselves, they saw a tiny, pleasant-looking man facing them. The man smiled in a friendly way at his two visitors. Then he nodded at the twins, and they moved closer to the car.

"So you're Mr Big," said Sally.

"Yes, yes, but it's Bigge — B.I.G.G.E." the man answered. "Please, no jokes about my name. I've heard them all. In fact, let's not talk about me at all. Let's talk about you. Tell me why you're following me. If I like what you say, I'll let you go back to that tin can of yours. If I don't – well, we'll have to work out something else."

He smiled as he spoke, but the look seemed frozen on his face. Sally could see that he would never believe anything they told him. But it looked like Jason wanted to try anyway.

"We know Lizzie Sloane," Jason said quickly. "We found out about your protection game and thought we'd try to talk our way in. We're good at the business. What do you say?"

"I say forget it," Mr Bigge answered, the smile still on his face. But then the smile dimmed. "I say you two are probably working for this Lizzie Sloane. Now get out of the car."

Jason and Sally climbed out as fast as they could. But the guns the twins were holding stayed pointed right at them. What a mess, Sally thought. Then she heard what Mr Bigge was saying to his helpers.

"Having those two around is bad for my health. I want them done away with now – quickly and quietly. And get rid of that junk car too."

The twins waved their guns at Jason and Sally, and the four started walking into the woods. In a moment, Mr Bigge's car drove away. Jason hadn't heard the orders, but it was easy to see that he had guessed what was happening.

Come on, Barzak, Sally thought wildly as she looked at Jason's worried face. You made my mind work better before. Please put another good idea into it! But nothing came to her. She just kept on walking, hearing the snap of branches breaking under her feet.

Then suddenly she thought of something. The woods were full of fallen trees. If she could lift a car, she could lift a tree trunk — and swing it at the twins. They'd be too surprised to get out of the way.

"When I trip, hit the ground fast," she whispered to Jason. "What are you talking about?" he asked.

"Just do it," she told him.

"Cut the talk," one of the twins called out.

"Now," said Sally. She tripped and fell, and Jason came down next to her. Bullets sailed over them as Sally grabbed hold of a giant trunk. But it didn't move.

"Run," Jason called as the twins jerked their

guns back and forth trying to decide where to fire next. It was too late to do anything more about the tree trunk. Sally went diving for cover.

She landed behind the tree next to where Jason was hiding. Bullets flew around them. "Are you crazy?" Jason asked her, ducking down low to the ground. "You were trying to pick up a tree trunk. What were you planning to do? Build a house?"

"Forget it," Sally said. "I just thought I had a good idea."

She needed one now. The bullets were coming closer with every shot.

"I think that's eight," Jason called.

"Eight what?"

"Bullets. Shots. They can't have more than 12 between them. Our friends are carrying Colts, and those guns hold only six shots each. If we can make them shoot, they'll run out and have to load up again. Let's start moving. And as soon as they stop firing, we'll make a dash for the car."

They began diving from tree to tree. Pretty soon Sally could see the Ford on the road through the trees.

"This way," she called to Jason. Shots rang out around him.

"Nine, ten," he counted.

Then they saw a giant rock only a few yards away. But to reach it, they would have to cross an open space.

"Do you think you can make it to that rock?" Jason asked.

Sally nodded.

They went racing for the rock. Both guns went off as the two runners slid behind it and out of danger. "Eleven, twelve," Jason said and smiled.

They were safe now. Without wasting time, Sally and Jason went crashing through the last patch of woods to the Ford.

It started up before the twins could make it to the road. But it didn't sound very good. "I've got an idea," Sally said. She jumped out of the Ford and ran around it to the Mercedes.

"I hope it's not lifting tree trunks again," Jason called. That stopped Sally cold. She had figured she could push the Mercedes into the ditch. But now she knew that Jason would ask her too many questions.

Instead, she bent down and let the air out of the Mercedes' front tyre. Then smiling, she climbed back into the Ford and drove away. Through the mirror, she saw the twins watching them.

* * *

A call to the police soon had Mr Bigge and the Spark twins locked up. And on Thursday afternoon, Sally and Jason went to Lizzie's to get their money.

"I wanted Mr Bigge first," Lizzie told them. "You didn't do as you were told."

"That's £400 a day plus," Sally said. "We're not moving out of here until we see our money."

Lizzie began to laugh. "You're a pretty tough customer youself, aren't you? I think you could turn this place inside out if you wanted to."

Sally smiled. "I think I could too."

"All right, I'll pay you," said Lizzie. "And stick around. I'll throw in dinner too."

"No dinner for me," said Sally. "I never bowl on a full stomach. Some other time, but not tonight."

"So that's what Thursday night is all about," Jason said.

"I'll see you tomorrow morning, bright and early," Sally told him.

CHAPTER

14

No Time to Spare

It was almost nine o'clock as Sally pushed open the doors of the bowling alley. She had been waiting for this moment all week. She smiled as she made her way through the noise of falling pins and shouts of excitement.

Then she remembered — on Thursdays all the lanes were saved for team use. Sally probably wouldn't be able to get one for herself. She looked around just in case. But as she had expected, every lane was taken.

Maybe someone on a team didn't show up, she thought. Maybe I can fill in for a missing player. Sally began to check the lanes. Soon she spotted four women throwing practice balls. They kept looking toward the door — for their other team member, Sally hoped.

"Are you short of a player?" Sally asked one of the women. She was dressed in a pink shirt that said Mel's Machine Shop across the back.

"We sure are," the woman answered. "If we don't have another player in five minutes, the team we're supposed to play wins without a fight. Are you interested in filling in?"

Sally nodded.

"Great. Are you a good bowler?"

"Does it matter?" Sally asked, laughing.

"It would be nice if you were," the woman told her. "But now we'd take any player."

Sally was grinning as she put her bowling shoes on. Then Judy Harper spotted her and walked over. They met at the ball return between lanes seven and eight.

"Are you bowling for this team now?" Judy asked. "I'm really glad to see you haven't given up."

"I'm playing with them just for tonight," Sally said. "They needed another player."

Judy smiled. "I'm glad you came. And I can see for myself now what Joe told me. You do look different. In fact, you look just great!"

Sally grinned. "Leaving that job — and a few other things — has made me a new person. Not being under Edna's shadow helps too." She looked back as someone on her team called to her. "I think I'm up now she said to Judy. "Talk to you later."

Sally picked up her bowling ball. It looked the same, but Sally knew it was different. This ball would never sweep a gutter again. After all, if she was quicker, stronger, and all those other things Barzak had made her, she was sure to be a better bowler.

Sally rolled many strikes for her first game — a lot more than she had ever had before. She thought hard and carefully about placing every ball. It was wonderful to end up with a score of 172.

Thank you, Barzak, Sally thought as the women on her team smiled and patted her on the back. Too bad I couldn't have done this well without Barzak's help. But at least I'm on top of things now.

Then the next game started. Sally bowled a strike in the first frame. Frames two, three, and four were strikes, too. Barzak, you're really going to town, Sally thought.

Now for frame five. Sally looked at the pocket and sailed the ball down the alley. Strike! People were starting to call over and wish her good luck. Six, seven, eight — three more strikes.

Sally didn't want to think ahead, but she could't help hoping. Was it possible she was on the way to a perfect game?

Frame nine. Here we go. Sally said to herself. She watched, hands on hips, as the ball headed for the pocket. Again the ball sailed in for a strike. It was too easy. She needed just three more strikes for a perfect game.

Sally picked up her ball at the ball return. She tried not to notice all the people who were watching her play. She rolled the ball — for another strike.

As the pins crashed down, an icy voice broke into her thoughts. "My, you have been practising!" Sally looked to see Edna standing next to her. She had come to join the crowd around Sally.

Suddenly Sally felt some of her control slipping away. "Uh, just a good night, I guess," she said. She had thought she would only feel sorry for Edna from now on. But it seemed the woman still had some power over her.

Quickly Sally picked up her ball and walked over to the line. She looked at the pins, and then sent the ball rolling. But half-way down the alley, it wobbled, curved, and dropped into the gutter. A groan went up from the crowd. The perfect game was ruined. Sally couldn't believe what had happened.

Barzak, she thought, what's going on? She went back to the ball return. Maybe I picked up the wrong ball, she said to herself. Maybe only the ball has special power and not me. But no. The ball that rolled back to her was her own. Shaken and surprised, Sally picked it up and headed back to the line. She had one last chance to knock down some pins.

Standing there Sally felt Edna watching her. And somewhere inside of herself, something said that she couldn't let Edna see her mess up again. She looked at the pins. Barzak or not, she thought, I'm going to knock some of them down.

She walked to the line and rolled her ball. It went straight down the lane without curving. Eight pins fell over. A small cheer went up. It might not have been a perfect game, but it certainly was a good one. At 278 it was better than anything Sally had ever done before.

There was one more game to play. Sally felt a little tired, but she tried hard. She rolled another good game, for Sally Steele — 168. But when she left the alley, she was mixed up. Why hadn't the near-perfect game been more exciting to roll, not just easy? For some reason, Sally found herself more pleased with the last game — when she had worked for every pin. What was going on?

CHAPTER

15

Better Than Ever

Sally got into her Ford and slowly started for home. As she drove, she thought about the last few days. It seemed the things that had gone perfectly had been far less exciting than the things that had not. If her life was going to be just the way she wanted, would it be terribly dull and no fun at all?

She turned onto Sherman Drive thinking about the old Sally Steele. That Sally had always dreamed about things getting better without trying to make them better. Now the new Sally Steele had everything going for her. Yet deep down, she seemed to be hoping that things would return to the way they used to be. Suddenly a loud noise broke into her thoughts and the Ford's engine cut out. Oh, no, Sally thought. Not again — and not here.She steered off the road. With a tired groan, she leaned back in the seat and looked out of the window.

What —? Could it be? A circle of blue lights was shining above her. She watched it start down toward her.

"Oh, let it be Barzak," Sally said to herself as she stepped out of the car.

She watched the strange spaceship land again in the centre of Sherman Drive. Then the side door opened. But this time, something green and round with 10 arms rolled out and up to Sally.

"Oh, you're not Barzak," Sally thought as she watched the creature.

The answer formed in Sally's mind. "But I am Barzak. I'm just 100 years older, that's all. I think turning green is nicer than turning grey, don't you?"

"Never mind that," Sally thought, taking Barzak by two arms. "I have to talk to you." She stopped suddenly. "What do you mean, 100 years older?"

"Just what I said. I'm wearing out. But then so are you."

"Wait a second," Sally sent her message quickly. "Hold everything. You promised me 100 years — but of *my* time, I thought."

"I never said whose time," Barzak told her. "I'm afraid I meant mine. Couldn't you tell that your parts were beginning to wear out sometime yesterday afternoon?"

"Yesterday afternoon? Impossible," Sally said. "I managed to escape from two killers. And you should have seen me bowl just a little while ago. The new me wasn't wearing out then, and it's not going to."

Barzak looked at her sadly with all four eyes. "I'm afraid it's already begun to. I'm sorry you didn't understand. I'm glad I was passing by and could stop down to tell you."

"It's not fair," said Sally. "I thought you meant 100 years of Earth time. What good is a week?"

"Some people could do wonders in a week," Barzak told her. "In fact, I think you have. You're looking very well. Of course, you'd look better if you were blue and had a few more arms. But it seems you've had an interesting time. And you've held up very well. But now you're on your own." The old creature turned and started back to its ship.

Sally sat down on the side of the road. She was so surprised she could only watch as Barzak rolled into the ship and headed off into the night. Some hundred years, Sally thought. But then she thought some more. Even though her week was over, she was still a different Sally Steele from the one she had been. And already had done a lot of things on her own. Now maybe she would do more — and make her life work the way she wanted it to.

Sally smiled to herself as she stood up. Then with a quick step, she started to walk the two miles home.